A Path Between Houses

The Brittingham Prize in Poetry

THE UNIVERSITY OF WISCONSIN PRESS POETRY SERIES

RONALD WALLACE, GENERAL EDITOR

A Path

BETWEEN

Houses

For Daisy —
Whose work I loved coming in,
and whom I love walking away
from this place. Please stay in
touch!

Greg Rappleye

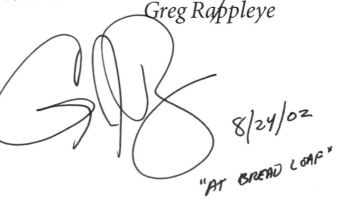

8/24/02

"AT BREAD LOAF"

The University of Wisconsin Press

The University of Wisconsin Press
2537 Daniels Street
Madison, Wisconsin 53718

3 Henrietta Street
London WC2E 8LU, England

5   4   3   2   1

Printed in the United States of America

Library of Congress Cataloging-in-Publication-Data
Rappleye, Greg
A path between houses / Greg Rappleye.
    pp. cm.—(The Brittingham prize in poetry)
ISBN 0–299–17010–1 (cloth: alk. paper)
ISBN 0–299–17014–4 (pbk.: alk. paper)
I. Title. II. Brittingham prize in poetry (Series)
PS3568.A6294 P38   2000
811'.6—dc21   00–010299

For

  Hannah & Elliot

and for

  Marcia Kennedy Rappleye

"Do you know, Quincy, I've often wondered whether there isn't more in the old legend of the Garden of Eden, and so on, than meets the eye. What if Adam wasn't really banished from the place at all? That is, in the sense we used to understand it—" The walnut grower had looked up and was fixing him with a steady gaze that seemed, however, directed at a point rather below the Consul's midriff—"What if his punishment really consisted," the Consul continued with warmth, "in his having to go on living there, alone, of course—suffering, unseen, cut off from God . . . Or perhaps," he added, in a more cheerful vein, "perhaps Adam was the first property owner and God, the first agrarian, a kind of Cardenas, in fact—tee hee!—kicked him out. Eh? Yes," the Consul chuckled, aware, moreover, that all this was possibly not so amusing under the existing historical circumstances, "for it is obvious to everyone these days—don't you think so, Quincy?—that the original sin was to be an owner of property . . ."

—Malcolm Lowry, *Under the Volcano*

If you don't know how, I'll show you how to walk the dog.

—Rufus Thomas

CONTENTS

III

ACKNOWLEDGMENTS

Grateful acknowledgment is made to the editors of those publications in which the following poems, some in slightly different form, originally appeared:

Artful Dodge: "The Assistant Prosecutor's Story"
Louisiana Literature: A Review of Literature and the Humanities: "At Forty-Seven Days"
Mississippi Review: "Homer, Faulkner, *Noir*" and "From The Vegas Cantos"
Prairie Schooner: "Mythe," "Walking Toward the Village," and "Walk-away"
Puerto del Sol: "Broken Neck"
Quarterly West: "Bone Island in Summer"
Santa Barbara Review: "Cat Descending a Staircase"
Southern Review: "Terrible," "Cause," "Calling the Code," and "Wanted: Japanese Sword"
Sou'Wester: "The Far-Away Rivers," "Dusk," and "Hornets' Nest"
Spillway: "A Path Between Houses"
Sycamore Review: "Charon in August"
Watershed: "Morning at the Artist's House, Key West," "At the Ice Dock," and "Comet"

"Fidelity" appeared, and "Terrible" and "Charon in August" were reprinted in *New Poems from the Third Coast: Contemporary Michigan Poetry*
"Homer, Faulkner, *Noir*" and "From The Vegas Cantos" won *The Mississippi Review Prize in Poetry*
"From The Vegas Cantos" was reprinted in *The Pushcart Prize XXV: Best of the Small Presses*

I am forever indebted to the faculty, staff, and students of the M.F.A. Program for Writers at Warren Wilson College, and especially to Anne

Winters, Mary Leader, Lucia Perillo, and Brooks Haxton. I thank the best writing group that ever was, *The Amazing Spunky Monkeys:* Jane Bach, Jack Ridl, and Heather Sellers, who worked patiently through the many drafts of these poems. My debt to my wife Marcia is incalculable—first reader, best critic, and fierce defender. *When I count the things that are in my heart, you are what counts the most.*

I

Homer, Faulkner, *Noir*

"Oh, you are odd, I see."
INO TO ODYSSEUS, Book V, *The Odyssey*

How the modern *noir* resembles the ancient *noir.*
The war is over. Odysseus, adrift since leaving
Calypso, on his way home. Lost in a storm,
he is visited by Ino, former mortal,
now a minor goddess, who, like a Hollywood starlet,
has changed her name, in this case
because her husband was a murderer.
Don't ask. The myths are so complex.
Anyway, she lands on his raft
in the form of a gannet. Odd enough,
even in those ancient days when a seabird might
land on a raft, sweet tangle in her beak
(which becomes a magic cloak), and begin
talking, like a smart-aleck waitress
in a desert roadhouse. But Ino speaks the words
so quietly, Homer barely writes them.
Of every translation I've read, only Rouse
nurses them from the text. Even Odysseus
isn't sure what she says, hesitates,
is seen by Poseidon before he can escape,
and the poem goes on, dark and inexplicable,

        like the plot to *The Big Sleep,*
Faulkner brought in by Howard Hawks
to make some sense of it, to "punch it up,"
and Faulkner makes it better, but more confusing,
until Hawks, watching the final cut, despairs,
and tells Faulkner, who is on his way to
Rowan Oak, to write one more scene and
he'll bring back the stars (Bogart & Bacall)
to film it. And he *will,* time and again, trying

starlet after starlet in the scene's crucial role,
until Patricia Clarke finally gets it right: It is night
outside a shed in the desert. Marlowe fires his gun,
the smoke licking the fender of his Ford
coupe. Sapped from behind and *cut,*
we see him, coming-to, captive of Eddie Mars'
wife, who needs to know what Howard Hawks can't
figure out: What has Eddie Mars done and what
is his link to Sean Regan? So Marlowe tells her,
Your husband is a murderer, and she slaps him,
hard, and walks out of the room. *She's all right,*
Marlowe says, rubbing his cheek, *I like her.*

And so does Faulkner, who finishes the scene
at 3 A.M., on the Missouri Pacific
just west of Memphis. He takes a last sip
of bourbon and branch water, kisses the script
for luck, shoves it into an envelope,
and shambles out to find the porter, a man,
shiny and black, who slides around the club car
like St. Elmo's fire. Faulkner tells him
to mail the envelope at the next stop
and hands him a silver dollar. *Yes, sir,*
the porter says, and at Memphis
steps off the train, drops the packet
into the box, turns and flips
the silver dollar, a coin so heavy and slow
he counts the spins—*five, six, seven,* then snaps it
from the air, the back of his black hand
beginning to sweat, shining brighter than
the coin it covers. Across the platform, a soldier
lights a smoke and mumbles something
vile, because he is drunk and because
a black man isn't supposed to have a silver dollar
in the State of Tennessee. *What did he say?*
The porter misses a step, his skin beginning to burn,
then shakes it off, laughs and gets back on the train.

4

It is 1946. The war is over. It is the cusp
of the Postmodern Era. The porter knows it is
all aboard this train that is leaving, all aboard
this train that is going home.

Mercywood

Mother is driving me from one insecurity
to another in a silver Mercury,
tail fins tailing through the darkness.
"You'll never know what I went through
so you could be born," she says
and takes another drink. It is the middle
of a night in 1958. Precocious reader, I
have a picture book of outer space,
and as we pass the headlights of a car,
I flash upon a future in the dark:
a spaceship, pointy and finned, rocketing
across the galaxy, or a spaceman mapping
a dusty red planet. That's when we see
the glowing red sign—MERCYWOOD, floating
above a vagueness on the right. Mother says
she'll drag me there the next time I go nuts.
"They'll pack you in oil and run juice
through your veins, they'll give you shots
to make you sleep." Red glow suffuses
the asylum grounds, and Mother says
the light is red so crazy people think
they are dangling in the Sweet Heart of Jesus.
"Red air looks exactly like Christ's
diaphanous blood." I am directly behind her
now. We are steering the same course,
over-driving the high beams, both of us
staring through the wheel to know where
we are going, the Mercury hurtling past
the dark side of the asylum. We fly by
all the other cars. In the northern sky,
the dipper stands on its handle-end.

At such an angle, could the charts read
anything but emptiness? Every star is
white.

Wild Irish: 1959

It might have been my father, saying
to the black man's wife, *That dress looks
nice,* and her saying back something
flirtatious. Things not said between
a black woman and white man
in Jackson, Michigan, not
in the "changing" neighborhood east
of Francis Street, brick bungalows and
three-bedroom two-stories, just four blocks
from a row of black-and-tans.

Whatever happened, Mother drank
all week, and on Friday afternoon,
fueled by *Four Roses* and her inability
to make Father *tell the whole truth,*
stood by the forsythia bush
and hurled the phrase, *Black bitch!*
into the neighbor's yard, the words
landing, like a bottle of gasoline
at the feet of the woman next door,
as she carried groceries into her house.

The two women stood at the frontier
of the yards, slapping and pulling
each other's hair, then the black woman
yanked mother's tube top down,
and mother's breasts swung free
in the heavy August air. Who was first,
then, to raise a knife? I can't say.
Mother ran for the house,
her chestnut hair flying, breasts still
not tucked into her top, and

came back with a cleaver in her hand,
and then the black woman stood
in her yard, flailing her arms, eyes
wide, holding an open straight-edge.
Mother was yelling *Nigger whore!*
and the black woman called Mother
a *white-trash peckerwood cunt,*
the meaning of which I couldn't guess,
six-years-old and peeking above
the rickety front-porch rail.

No one was cut. No blood was spilled.
Mr. Davis must have heard the screams
from his workshop, because he brought
a dowel he'd been turning on his lathe.
Then Mrs. Mytelka, the Polish woman
who lived at the end of the street, who made
the most delicious potato pancakes,
came running, and pulled Mother
back from the drive. No one dared
step into the black woman's yard,

telling her from the safety of the walk
to get into her house, Mother yelling,
with the circular thoughts and thick tongue
of the hopelessly drunk, that her uncle
was with the police, and if the police were
called, there would be trouble.
Father came home and found her
passed out on the living-room couch.
Within a week, our house was for sale,
and then we moved to the other side

of town, a place where, Mother proudly
said, "We could live with our own kind,"
that arrogant breed of priests, cops, and

distillery men, skilled at bartending
and curbside engine repair, who, in another age,
painted themselves blue and rolled down the hills
of Donegal, who waggled spears and genitalia
to frighten their enemies, and after the battle,
gathered round the fires to celebrate the fight,
expecting their poets to sing of it.

Thousand Dollar Days

The man at the picnic table
in front of the root beer stand
in northern Michigan is my father.
Do you see his sign,
twirling through the piney air?
There are two hours until he opens,
and he's drinking a cup of black coffee,
making a list for the salesman
from the wholesale grocery,
who'll be banging at the backdoor
after the noontime rush. The sun
angles from the gas station and across
the parking lot,
where crows compete for popcorn
dropped by last night's customers,
mostly teenage kids,
on vacation with their parents
from the suburbs of Detroit.
It's the summer after the summer
their city burned. Martin is dead and Bobby is
dead, and Nixon is yet to come,
Denny McLain is flaming his way to 31 wins,
and America thrashes in the bed
of Southeast Asia. But in a tourist town,
traffic is what matters.
So my father lays his pen down
to watch the passing cars, subtracting out
the junky Fords and pickups of the locals.
Inside, the hired woman wipes a rag along the counter
and begins to sing a hymn,
her voice carrying through the screens
and rolling sweetly below the canopy
that shelters as many as fourteen cars

on rainy afternoons. My father's eyes
are gin-clear, and he's sketching out plans
to add barbecue after the Fourth of July.
He counts three good car hops,
four sons and two daughters,
old enough to hold their own
through the heaviest dinner hour.
The season hasn't really begun,
but already he's had thousand dollar days.
My father smiles. His lot is
full, he imagines the rush,
as his hand strikes something
from his list. And I'm the skinny boy
you see, arms and legs furiously churning,
rounding the corner from the old highway
to the new, sprinting toward the pylon
that rises from that one-story building
like a jagged orange fin, who sees his father smiling
and believes, against all the evidence,
that he might be the reason why.

Broken Neck

I remember adjusting the choke,
pulling the cord, the deadhead I chose
to stun the aluminum boat.
The empty shell laid down a circle
of smoke, and whatever happened
was visible to the one
who found my body drifting
somewhere above the lake bed.
Mother showed up drunk
in her dusty station wagon.
This family is like the goddamned
Walendas! she said to the men above me,
as she began the task
of slapping me back to life.
Because I wouldn't move,
Mother mixed a gin and tonic
and drove me wild through the tourist towns.
Light wheeled through the windows,
my body curled
into a smaller, more delicate body,
and Mother jabbered about love and paralysis,
all the way to the hospital doors.
Look what I've got!
she told the attendants,
as they strapped my body down,
my good hand grasping and then
letting go. I was naked beneath
the crisp white sheets,
my skin electric,
the glassine membrane of a concussion
just now peeling back. I didn't know
if I could move, but I heard a man

pushing my body toward the machine.
Something was broken inside me,
and they were sure to find it.

Collar Cut

It's the moment semiotics begins
to make sense. A man thinks *salmon*
in a dimly lit fish house, as a chute feeds
dead king after dead king, which he takes,
one-by-one from the water-wash,
and inserts into a heading machine,
the pneumatic < of the blade thunking
down and through to separate head
from body—a *collar cut,* just behind
the gills. It isn't his job to sort males,
(plum-red, hook-jawed, thick with
grayish clots of milt), from females,
(evergreen, honey-combed with
golden roe). He simply thinks *salmon*
and slides the body forward, steps
to trigger the device, then the pneumatic
< drops like a rapid sigh, and the head falls
or is cleared by the women
on the cleaning line, who will take
the headless body, razor the belly, and
if it is female, drop the eggs
into a bucket, then pass the fish
to the gutting crew. The man works on, until
he sees *gloved hand* and thinks *salmon*
and the pneumatic < drops and cuts
glove, flesh, and bones an inch above the wrist
in a perfect collar cut, more quickly than
signs arrange vowels and consonants
in his mind, and the hand falls
into a box of bloody salmon heads,
bound for sale as crab bait. He
reaches with what is left, still wearing
the cuff of the yellow glove

like a bracelet, and doesn't think
hand until blood comes in two quick
pumps, splattering into the box of dead
kings, as lights start to spin and
the women look up from their work,
knives gleaming.

Setting Nets Near Cypremort Point

The hand is quicker than the eye.
CARNIVAL SAYING

Almost midnight. Moth-moon and bright stars. Details that count, because mullet move on this moon. Billy and Ed Curry are drunk. Their kicker boat is tied to Walter's *Miss Colleen,* a forty foot gill-netter out of Cortez. To the starboard and lee, running lights and radio traffic, the occasional mutter of an exhaust. The Cajuns don't like us. The Currys and Walter are Florida bay men. I'm worse, *a Yankee,* here to buy roe mullet. But we have permits, and we're rafted at the mouth, waiting for the bayou to open. Walter tolerates me because the man I work for holds the paper on his boat. The Currys, because I pay cash for roe. Metallic and sour, it's sold in Taiwan as an aphrodesiac. *You pay a price for what you believe.* The Currys are crushing beer cans, then swatting them off the transom. "You got any cash?" Ed asks me, "Or'd you spend it all on that whore in Chalmette?" The truth is, there wasn't any whore in Chalmette, but what's true isn't easy for Ed. *Oh, I've got money,* I tell him. "Let's see it," Billy says, an edge in his voice. "Is it in that bag?" Meaning the sample case I stowed forward as we left the dock. I look at Walter. Part of him needs to see it, too. I get the case, open the latch, reach in, slide the clip home and safety off, and come up with a 9 mm automatic. I aim the pistol toward them, moonlight firing the satin-black finish, index finger curled round the trigger, giving them the look they asked for, as the Curry brothers stand and head for their boat.

Terrible

The man from room 8
is washing and waxing his car.
It's a black Ford, with flames
stenciled on the doors,
and the word *Terrible*
inscribed in an elegant cursive
on the pillars of the roof.
I think I know his life. I lived it
at Red's Motel, on a stinky bayou
near Hopedale, Louisiana.
We called it "Hopeless,"
as in, "Maybe I'll call you,
when I get back to Hopeless."
It was a bad place, full of oil workers
and helicopter pilots.
I was driving the coast
in a rental sedan, setting up deals
to cut and pack fish. I carried
a leather sample case,
a book of account,
and a 9 mm Glock
with two fully loaded clips.
No one believes the part about the gun.
But there are things I did
you wouldn't necessarily believe.
The truth is, I only fired it once.
I bought twelve honey rock melons
and a six-pack of beer
in Pascagoula, Mississippi.
"I'm having a picnic," I told the clerk,
and drove out to a swampy field
near the Pascagoula River.
A 9 mm Glock will flat play hell

on a honey rock melon.
Sometimes at night I'd lie in bed,
insects tapping against the screens,
drinking whiskey and cleaning the gun.
I didn't mind Red's Motel,
and I didn't mind carrying the Glock,
and if a situation arose,
I would have used it.
So what happened? I can't say.
Let's suppose a moment of clarity
in a burning cane field
outside New Iberia,
where someone finally realized
the man he worked for
was a terrible man.
I tossed the Glock off the ferry
that crosses the Mississippi
between Vacherie and Lutcher.
And now I'm six doors down
from room 8.
So I remember what it's like,
living in a bad place,
cleaning and polishing the one thing
you know will get you home.
The allegiance you build to it,
day after terrible day.

Porpoise

There was a seafood restaurant
on the north shore. I used to walk over
after the restaurant closed. They had
a dock, and a trawler tied to pilings
that rocked as boats passed, lines
singing against wood. In the water
was a cage, though it was open
at the deep end, and she could swim away
any time she wanted. I'd bring a mullet,
or a small grouper from which I'd cut
the sharper fins. The water was dark,
but I could hear her, swirling after a fish
or kicking to the bottom of her pen.
Then she'd roll beside the dock
and watch with one oleaginous
eye, turning every so often to take in
and expel great lung-fulls of air. She
was a good listener. I'd lie on the dock
and stare at the stars, going on
about the different kinds of loneliness.
I was drinking then and couldn't say
when we began swimming together.
She had a sweetness, though, letting me
hold her dorsal fin and coming up to nudge
my belly or my side. The Gulf was warm,
and there were nights I saw the moon
as a blurry monotype and felt the pull
of a running tide. That was years ago.
She must be dead now. I mean,
how long can a porpoise live?
But it was something, how she cared

for me. Bringing me up for air,
pushing me toward the dock
when she knew I'd had enough.

My Communist Years

On an afternoon in the fall of 1969,
the Socialist Workers came
to mobilize the proletariat
of Jackson, Michigan—the sweet idiots
who made brakes at Kelsey Hayes and tires
at the tire factory. As protests go,
it wasn't much: one hundred true believers
in the park across the street, stirred
by a ragged man with a bull horn.
They began to move on the Armory,
chanting *One, two, three, four!*
We don't want your fucking war!
My father, who spent the last days
of August 1945, deployed to pack lettuce
under the cloudless skies of Salinas, California,
clenched his fists and I suddenly knew
life was dull compared to death
in Southeast Asia. So I ran to join the march.
My father came after me, yelling,
You goddamned commie! So yes, I am
there, in the photograph on page one
of the *Citizen Patriot*—the boy with the buzzy haircut,
running toward the lens,
bug-eyed, mouth open as though he is hungry.
Perhaps that is my father's arm,
behind the earnest woman in braids
raising her fist in the air,
his body lost among the other bodies.
Can you hear the voices chanting, or even
a single voice? This is the old story, it is
a *dialectic*, and the words
coming from my father's mouth
are wind over his teeth.

At the Ice Dock

November comes near the mouth
of the river. I've driven down
from New Orleans, to haggle
the price that must be paid
to get mullet iced, boxed, and
free-on-board, bound for Pascagoula.
Near the mooring lines,
an orange forklift accelerates
and retreats.

They are unloading tuna
from *The Mother of Jesus,*
a longliner out of Mandeville.
Miles of line circle the reels.
Hundreds of blaze-orange floats
crowd her foredeck, like refugees
from a cautious land.
I squat down to touch a yellowfin
laid out by the dock workers.
The pupil of its yellow eye
is a black disc. A streak of yellow disappears
along its side, then appears again
in the fins and finlets
that stretch along the back
and underbelly, like the savage teeth
of an ancient hacksaw.

Last night, I drank until
I could no longer calculate,
then wandered through the rainy streets
of the French Quarter.
Black men with trumpets,
tubas, saxophones, and drums,

huddled under awnings, pressed
into alcoves and sheltered alleys,
stepping in place
to a slow and mournful jazz.
The crowd stood motionless,
and the Halloween costumes
grew horrific in the rain.

Here, the packing goes on.
The tuna are weighed, flesh
is cored. Each fish is boxed,
laid out on ice. Each box,
the size of a small coffin.
The dock crew close and band them,
then stack the boxes, one atop
another. The forklift does its work.
Beyond the dock and across the dead air,
the day is moving slowly
toward the impossible blue
of the Gulf.

From The Vegas Cantos

"Hey, I like to swing as much as anybody,
but this ain't a plan, it's a pipe load of the crazy stuff."
DEAN MARTIN, from the original shooting script for *Ocean's Eleven*

January 1960. Klieg lights, Sinatra
at the Sands, filming underway
for the Rat Pack movie, the Strip
blazing neon. The plot, such as it is:
Eleven ex-soldiers, led by Frank,
rob five casinos on New Year's Eve
after Sammy knocks out the power lines.
Every day, the production shoots into dusk.
Cesar Romero as Duke Santos
trying to intimidate the boys,
Sammy driving the truck full of money
through the Sheriff's blockade,
Angie Dickinson telling Ilka Chase
just how it is between Angie and Frank,
how it's always going to be, five different bands
playing "Auld Lang Syne," over and over,
dancing into The New Frontier.
It's hard work and at night they unwind
with vodka martinis, a bottle
of Jack Daniel's, a splash of soda,
unfiltered Chesterfields. *Smoking is all
in the wrist,* Lawford says.

⋆   ⋆   ⋆

At 1 A.M.,
Frank backs away from the piano
in the Copa Room, says, *The action here
is getting old,* to Sammy, Sammy nods at Dean,
the Pack rises, pushes toward the exit.

In the parking lot, three El Dorado
convertibles: one pearlescent blue,
one lemon chiffon, one green mist,
all courtesy of Jack Warner.
They load the cars, tops down.
It's January in the desert, but a warm front
has burgeoned up from the Sea of Cortez,
and Dean says, *It's rag top weather, baby,*
nudging the strapless breasts
of a showgirl's sequined gown.
Frank and Dean in front, Angie, Ilka,
then Sammy driving the chiffon El Dorado,
Lawford sipping a traveler, more girls,
Joey Bishop, the only sober one,
driving the third car and *worried,* Romero,
drunk and laughing, Shirley McClaine
and another chick in back. *Does Frank know
where he's going?* Joey wants to know.
It's your job to be the mother! Romero says.
And too often, Joey thinks, *Right,* I'm the one
left paying for broken windows
and slipping fifty to the maitre d'
while the others scoot through the kitchen,
playing pat-ass on the way. Behind
the third Cadillac, the parking attendant,
Paco, drives his '53 Chevy pickup—
Richard Conte, already swan-songed
in the movie, (*Your guy buys the big casino,*
Frank had explained), flat-drunk
in the bed of the truck, Henry Silva,
Norman Fell, and a couple of broads
holding stakes that rise from the sides,
everyone singing *Come Fly With Me,*
Frank's number-one hit.

                *   *   *

                    On they go,
ten, twenty miles into the desert,
until Romero begins to wonder if this is
such a good idea, until the singing stops
and the girls have started to shiver.
Dean lights another cigarette, looks
sideways at Frank, who has said almost nothing.
Just as Dean is about to ask, *What's up, amigo?*
Frank goes, *This is the place,* jerks the car
onto a two-track, bottoms through the alkali flats
and drives on. Sammy,
his good eye almost hypnotized
by the dashing lines of U.S. 95,
comes to, chases the pearlescent blue
El Dorado off the road,
the green Cadillac and flat-gray pickup
follow suit. Frank finally stops, hops out,
his car in park, headlights still on.
Circle up! he yells, looping a finger
in the air. Frank backs the drivers off,
making sure they leave enough space
in the middle. Everyone piles out.
Paco! Frank snaps, *You and Normie*
grab some branches off that pile of mesquite!
Dean, Sammy, get the booze and blankets
outta the trunk. You girls, there's a cooler
and snacks in the yellow El Dorado.
And while you're up, Dean,
tune the radios to that Mexican station
we've been listening to!
Sammy squirts the mesquite
with lighter fluid, tosses a match,
the oily flames rise into the sky,
the radios begin three hours of Basie,
Ellington, and Dorsey, between songs
the announcer hawking headache powders,
Geritola and *laxantes.*

*　*　*

A chill in the air. Stars swirl overhead,
miles from the neon clutter of the Strip.
Some pair off under blankets.
Sammy has a few drinks, smokes,
takes a chick he's been eyeing
into the lemon El Dorado. Her head
disappears, Sammy lies back
against the creamy leather.
You are the craziest, he says, over and over.
Dean chases Shirley around the fire.
She lets him catch up, paw her, stick his tongue
down her throat, bending her
in the crook of his left arm, martini balanced
in one hand, cigarette in the other.
Baby, he says, *let's rehearse our scene.*
She laughs, pushes him away, the pursuit begins
again.

*　*　*

Night goes by. Constellations rise.
Paco tends the fire, Romero falls asleep,
Norman Fell nods off, Silva wanders away,
Sammy snores in the El Dorado,
the sweet head of a showgirl in his lap.
"How Are Things in Glocca Morra?"
"Take the 'A' Train,"
"Ac-cent-tchu-ate the Positive,"
50,000 watts of Ensenada clear-channel
play on. Only Frank, Angie,
and Joey stay awake, Frank listening
to music, pacing, singing a scrap of lyric,
cupping a cigarette to his face,
pushing a black Panama snap-brim
back on his head, occasionally lighting

a Chesterfield for Angie. A sweet smell is
in the air, a redolence Frank knows
from the early forties—
the bad boys in the saxophone section.
Frank looks toward the pickup.
He sees the glow: Paco, Dean, and Lawford
passing a pipe of mary jane,
wacky tabacky, the crazy stuff.
Frank frowns. They're in the desert, okay,
no one around and if you stay clear
of the Mormons, anything goes,
but he doesn't need any hopheads
hanging around, capisce?
He looks at Angie, nods toward
the pickup, she shakes her head
in disapproval. *Take care of it,* Frank snaps
at Joey, then turns and walks
to the other side of the fire.

*   *   *

Stars turn. The fire burns down.
Frank looks at his watch. Almost 6 A.M.
He tells Joey, *Radios off. And roust Dean*
outta the truck, he's got to see this.
Frank steps fifty yards into the desert.
A few minutes later, Joey and Angie follow.
Dean, his head pounding, stumbles toward them.
Suddenly, the horizon ignites—soundless,
a half-moon of orange, yellow, and white fire
swells in the distance. Frank's face flashes
in the ignited air, he squints, heads jerk
back in alarm, a reaction to light,
Oh my God, Angie mouths, and Joey and Dean
just stand there. The blankets stir.
Sammy's head wobbles,
his good eye opens, a sleepy head

rises from his lap. Paco moans to consciousness,
begins to cross himself,
and before he gets to *Espiritu Santo*,
a windstorm sweeps through—
dust glows red below
the expanding mushroom cloud,
a concussion washes their bodies,
the earth begins to roll.
Everyone is awake now—even Conte's head rises
behind the pickup's cab.
To the east, the air is on fire, electric
with the bomb's ignition.
That's what I brought you to see,
Frank says, *the Big Kahplowie!*
raising a glass of bourbon
toward the towering firestorm,
Salud to Armageddon! he yells into the dust, turns
and tells everyone, *Pack it in*
before the fallout hits! He throws the keys
of the blue El Dorado at Dean.
You're sober. Drive. Joey,
take the yellow one. Lawford, the green.
Paco drives his own. Angie, you ride with me.
The caravan sets out. Conte stirs again,
Silva wipes atomic dust from his eyes.

          *   *   *

       In the back of the blue El Dorado,
Sinatra curls into the fetal position, his head
nested in Angie's lap. She smooths his cheek,
his face softens in the courtesy lights.
The radio is off, Dean in front, smoking
and driving, the horizon beginning to glow
with the orange and streaky pink
of a bombed-out desert sunrise. Ahead,
the other-glow of the Strip. Dean

finishes a cigarette, looks at it for a second
then flicks it over the side. In the mirror,
he watches it bounce and spray sparks
across the road, until it disappears
in the headlight-wash of the lemon El Dorado.
He begins to sing his new song
from the movie, scatting it, arriving
at the chorus, tapping his fingers on the wheel.
Ain't that a kick in the head?
he sings, *Ain't that a kick in the head?*

II

Walkaway

He made a gesture as if waving,
but did not look back.
PAUL MARIANI, *Dream Song: The Life of John Berryman*

Bobby runs from the Day Room.
He's going to see the woman he loves,
he doesn't care what
the restraining order says.
I see him slapping the panic bar
on the door. This is years ago, a hard fall
in Michigan, where I'm six days sober
on an "involuntary commit,"
reading *77 Dream Songs*.
What kind of life was this?
A different life. Let's say for a while
balance was a problem.
Last night, Bobby got mad at Albert
for changing channels during
The Price is Right, and Albert,
who hangs fenders at the Assembly Division
when he isn't snorting coke,
lifted Bobby from the love seat
like a poorly stamped part,
and banged him against the wall.
Now Bobby's crossing the field,
and someone yells, "Get a nurse!"
I want to laugh, because
no one makes a move.
Then Albert walks through the door to the patio
and stands with his back to us,
hands on his hips. Maybe he's going
to bring Bobby back. Maybe he isn't.
I think of the blind leading the blind.
I remember the pit they fall into.

We are strangers,
not compadres, Mr. Bones.
I am the third man out the door.
Dusk. The moon is large and could be taken
for anything at all. I say it is whiskey,
rising to my lips.
Years from now a cop will tell me,
The crazies run on a full moon,
trying to explain the word *lunatic.*
Have you ever known something
but acted as if you didn't?
Last call. The scent of burning leaves,
a moth fluttering up
to bang against the glass.
My hands want Librium.
My veins order a vodka with a twist.
And the field will have a gorge,
a river below, almost frozen,
and a bridge made to sing
in a northwest wind,
from which one might step, vanishing
where the air begins.
Now is the time. The growing dark.
The endless stupid drone of it.

At Forty-Seven Days

for Don Iden

Not drinking, I spot a ten-pound king
in whiskey-colored water.
The salmon drops into a hole,
then visible at the selvedge of gravel,
drifts.
I stand at the thread, cast twenty times,
the last few yanked back
with shaky rips,
risking the salmon into root-tangle.
But there is tapping or a slight pull
as something takes the fly
and tries to clear, so I raise the rod
and set the hook.
The line stalls at midstream.
I lift again and lose my footing,
seeming to hear gravel, like an adult life,
slip away beneath my heel, then regain it,
the salmon at full run, deeply hooked,
a violent flash of plum and darkling silver,
slashing across light and stones.
I keep the rod up, dragged downstream,
stripping line, tossing lengths over my shoulder
in a tangled nest and play him out,
until he comes at the shallows
one eye skyed, gill flaps clattering.
He makes three shrugs and
a slow chewing motion, as I sink
my hand into his gills
and lift, then smash his skull
twice against a rock.
I carry the fish to the rise of the oxbow,
press a camera into the crook of a tree

and set the self-timer, snapping
a picture of me holding the dead king
in the air. The man in this photograph
wants a drink and has killed something
he did not set out to kill. Tonight, he will
grill the salmon in butter and foil, over a wet fire
made from a shattered packing crate,
after scraping out the intestines, gills, and milt
with his bloody hands, and not wash them,
because he wants blood on his hands
or is afraid to walk back to the river
in the rain-spitting dark. But he will not drink.
By God, he will not drink.

The Dynamo Patents

I, Nikola Tesla, subject of the emperor
of Austria, from Smiljan, Lika, edgy edge
of the empire, land of goat carts and
cabbage eaters, lately resident of Gotham,
called by Lorca a place of teeming anthills,
have invented useful improvements
for electric dynamos, of which the following
are examples, reference being had
to certain affidavits and charts,
attached and forming part of the same.

Yes I, Nikola Tesla, who wept with gypsies
at Zagreb, know-all and tell-all, victim
of the greed of Edison and Westinghouse,
enemy of Marconi, financial dolt,
bankrupt, laughing stock, shunned
by the *haute bourgeoisie*, snaggle-toothed
melancholic, absinthe drinker, victim
of persistent skin disorders, and night-
wandering insomniac, who lingered
near the duck ponds of Central Park,

who spun electricity from the thundering
American Falls, who lit The White City
at the Chicago World's Fair,
who wrote poems in my laboratory, legs
crossed, sitting calmly, while sixty-foot sparks
shattered the room, joining oxygen and oxygen
into stinking ozone, pioneer of the death ray
and trans-Atlantic radio, who took 500,000 volts
through my veins, amazing my guests,
then shook hands with all, the cuffs

of my dinner jacket still smoking, blue flames
licking my prematurely gray hair,

yes I, Nikola Tesla, who am building
a tower in the American West,
from which I will someday speak to stars
and to men, have made certain improvements,
rewinding the coils, magnetizing new cores,
straightening the lines,
improving the generation of power.
What I claim is modest enough:
that the wires are tightly wound, that
the rotors will spin in all directions
hissing fire like a Catherine wheel,
that I have bolted a double helix
onto every moving part, that
I can step into the paint, take the charge,
and draw the foul.

A Path Between Houses

Where is the dwelling place of light?
And where is the house of darkness?
Go about; walk the limits of the land.
Do you know a path between them?
Job 38:19-20

The enigma of August.
Season of dust and teenage arson.
The nightly whine of pickup trucks
bouncing through the sumac
beneath the Co-Operative power lines,
country & western booming from woofers
carved into the doors. A trace of smoke
when the wind shifts,
spun gravel rattling the fenders of cars,
the groan of clutch and transaxle,
pickup trucks, arriving at a friction point,
gunning from nowhere to nowhere.
The duets begin. A compact disc,
a single line of muted trumpet,
plays against the sirens
pursuing the smoke of grass fires.

*   *   *

I love a painter. On a new canvas,
she paints the neighbor's field.
She paints it without trees,
and paints the field beyond the field,
the field that *has* no trees,
and the upturned Jesus boat,
made into a planter,
"For God so loved the world . . ."
a citation from John, chapter and verse,

splattered across the bow.
The boat spills roses into the weeds.
What does the stray dog know,
after a taste of what is holy?
The sun pulls her shadow toward me,
an undulant shape that shelters the grass,
an unaimed thing.

                *   *   *

In the gray house, the tiny house,
in '52 there was a fire. The old woman,
drunk and smoking cigarettes, fell asleep.
The winter of the blizzard and her son
not coming home from the Yalu.
There are times I still smell smoke.
There are days I know she set the fire
and why.

                *   *   *

Last night, lightning to the south.
Here, nothing, though along the river
the wind upends a willow,
a gorgon of leaves and bottom-up clod
browning in the afternoon sun.
In the museum we dispute
the poet's epiphany call—
white light or more warmth?
And what is the Greek word for the flesh,
and the body apart from the spirit,
meaning even the body opposed to the spirit?
I do not know this word.
Dante claims there are pools of fire
in the middle regions of hell,
but the lowest circles are lakes of ice,
offering the hope our greatest sins

aren't the passions, but indifference.
And the willow grew for years
with no real hold upon the ground.

       * * *

How the accident occurred
and how the sky got dark:
Six miles from my house,
a drunk leaves the Holiday Inn
spins on 104 and smacks a utility pole.
The power line sparks
across the hood of his Ford
and illuminates the crazed spider web
of the windshield. His bloody tongue burns
with a slurry gospel. Around me,
the lights go down,
the way death is described
as armor crashing to the ground,
the soul having already departed
for another place. Was it his body I heard
leaning against the horn,
the body's final song, before the body
slumped sideways in the seat?

       * * *

When I was a child,
I would wake at night
and imagine a field of asteroids, rolling
across the walls of my room.
In fact, I've seen them,
like the last herd of buffalo,
grazing against the background of fixed stars.
Plate 420 shows the asteroid 433 Eros,
the bright point of light, at its closest approach
to light. I lose myself in Cygnus,

ancient kamikaze swan,
rising or diving to earth,
Draco, snarling at the polestar,
and Pegasus, stone horse of the gods,
ecstatic, looking one last time at home.

* * *

August and the enigma it is.
Days when I move in crabbed circles,
nights when I walk with Jesus through the fields.
What finally stands between us
and the world of flying things?
Mobbed by jays, the Cooper's hawk
drops the dead bird. It tumbles
beneath the cedar tree,
tiny acrobat of death,
a dead bird released
in a failed act of atonement.
A nest of wasps buzzing beneath the shingles,
flickers drilling the cottonwood,
jays, sparrows, the insistent wrens,
the language of birds, heads cocked,
staring moon-eyed through the air.
Sedge, asters, and fleabane,
red tins of gasoline and glowing cigarettes,
the midnight voice of a fourteen-year-old girl
wailing the word "blue" from the pickup's open doors,
illuminated by the dome light,
the sulphurous rasp of another struck match,
red flowers of sheep sorrel, common mulleins
and foxglove, goldenrod and chicory,
the dry flowers of late summer,
an exhaustion I no longer look at.

* * *

Time passes. The authorities
gather the wreckage, the whirr
of cicadas, and light dissembles the sky.
A wind shift, and the Cedar Creek fire
snaps the backfire line
and roars through the cemetery.
In the morning,
I walk a path between houses.
I cross to the water
and circle again, the redwings
forcing me back from the marsh.
Smoke rises from a fire
still smoldering along the power lines,
flaring and exhausting itself
in the shape of something lost.
Grass fires, fires through the scrub
of the clear-cut, fires in the pulpwood,
cemetery fires,
the powder of ash still untracked
beneath the enormous trees,
fires that explode the seed cones
on the pines, the smoke of set fires
and every good intention gone wrong,
scorching the monuments
above the graves of the dead.

Cause

The first time I got sober,
I went sixty days, which ended
in Laredo, with a woman who sold law books.
It was the day the Challenger
smashed into the sea.
We were sitting on a deck,
watching an open field
between the hotel and the river.
Campesinos were wading
the Rio Grande. I can't say why.
It was easy enough to cross at the bridge.
She asked, would you like to go across
and eat roast goat? So we did,
and drank mescal in a smoky bar
where every shot came
with a dead worm. It isn't good
to break two months' sobriety
with ten shots of mescal.
Plus the beer it took to wash down the goat.
Those bodies in the sea—
they were something to drink about,
I told her, though I didn't need
a cause. Once we began, there was
reason enough to drink.

The Assistant Prosecutor's Story

I must confess. I'm the one
who prosecuted those triple-X movies,
and the clerk who rented them out
to the undercover cops.
It was nothing personal.
Like Andrea and Nikki,
naughty Mr. Gorman,
and the other well-endowed stars,
I had my part to play, and
if you judged no more than
they were judged, I might still be free.
The first was the usual thing—
pink bodies rolling against pink bodies,
giant cocks crashing into wet cunts,
vibrators buzzing with plastic desire,
and the wiener yanked from the bunghole
at the climax of every scene.
And that's exactly how
I summarized it for the jury:
"The Intruder licks Andrea's vulva,
Andrea rolls and performs fellatio
on the Intruder, Andrea masturbates,
Andrea and the Intruder have intercourse,
and the nasty Intruder penetrates
Andrea's anus." And so it went.
Nikki and Andrea atop each other,
groping away,
the burning-candle vignette,
two men shagging Nikki and lovely Nikki moaning
that she's *having a wonderful time,*
as the policemen come
and the movie ends.
The second was more of the same.

Except for my favorite part,
when Mr. Gorman did the deed
with the tempestuous Lupe.
"A real Mexican spitfire,"
the guy at the gas station would have said
when I was a kid,
after letting out a low whistle,
like the sound a bird makes, hiding
in the tall grass. I'd seen it five or six times,
but even I gasped
when Lupe screamed out in court,
"Fuck me with that big thing, Mr. Gorman!"
And I repeated it for the jury,
to prove the serious artistic intent
of this film. It was the best closing argument
I ever gave—as if I were making love
to the jury. And I had the urge
to pull a match to a cigarette,
as the judge droned out his instructions.
But my lovers took just twenty minutes
to find the defendant not guilty.
That night, I wanted to stop by your house
and say, "I am lost,"
and wanted it to mean something.
Not what Lupe meant,
when Mr. Gorman shoved his huge cock
into her ass, as she squealed like a leaky tire
rounding a sharp corner. No.
I wanted it the way it used to be.
You shuddering the phrase, *I acquit you,*
as the world reeled away
outside your bedroom window.

Dusk

Sitting in the back yard,
reading about the various untruths—
the lie of extended consciousness,
the lie of interpretation. Knowing
there are others. Down the hill,
the lake greens in the declining light,
and those who have motorboats
move in and out of the launching ramp.
I remember the lines
from another man's poem:
When he touches you,
it will be with my hands.
In summer, the songbirds never know
when to quiet themselves,
singing on into the darkness.

Wanted: Japanese Sword

It's one of those lighted signs
you tow behind a truck. For years,
the man down the street has kept it in his yard—
as if a retired samurai might wander by
on his way to Lund's Hardware
or the Whippi Dip. Tonight, I sit out
in the moonlight. The neighbor is drunk,
his stereo loud, *You done me wrong,*
sung in a man's voice. The music
seems familiar, but it's not.

Moonlight has a strange effect.
In 1856, under a full moon,
James Jesse Strang,
the self-styled Mormon prophet,
ran a sword through his chief rival
on Beaver Island, declared himself King
of Michigan, and began a bloody rebellion
that didn't end until a frigate was sent
to put it down. And did you know
the Japanese saber combines
a European hilt with a Japanese blade?
It's forty inches long and weighs three pounds.
Of course, my neighbor may want
a *katana,* long-sword of the samurai.
"The human heart is unknowable," the poet
Tsurayuki wrote, "but in my birthplace,
the flowers smell the same as always."
The wind moves through the roses
that tangle in the fence, roses that are
a delicate pink in any light.

Did you ever want a different life?
When I did, I went into the fish business
and sold salmon roe to the Japanese.
Ikura, it was called, tiny eggs
that gushed from the razored salmon
like translucent orange moons.
I was going to be rich.
You lost your ass! my father laughed,
meaning I would never be the King of Michigan.

The music stops. My neighbor
comes into his yard and starts
banging a stick against the ground.
He begins a drunken dance, a dark figure
backed by a glowing sign—whirling,
jumping on one leg—he falls, rises, and
falls again, twirling the stick around
his head, groaning and shouting out.
Finally, he stumbles and does not rise, his body
lost in the cedar-shadowed dark.
What does it mean to *want* so badly
you dance in the glow of your own desire?
Sending a stick hissing through the sky,
pounding the earth until you disappear,
amazing no one but yourself?

Bone Island in Summer

The tourists disappear
and the sky arcs through the phases
of aquamarine, deepening to cobalt
in the heel of the afternoon.
The redolence of orchids
settles over the asphalt
and the blackbirds scream at us
from the banyan trees.
The repetition comforts.
We lie in the sun,
shop for sandals and trinkets,
and when an afternoon drags
read biographies and poems,
or sit through the rain
eating chips with *salsa verde.*
On Truman Street,
the compassionate Virgin
stands above the door
of the Star of the Sea Church.
Chameleons scramble
over algae-darkened cement,
and a woman with a shaved head
pursues an orange-and-white cat
around the convent grounds. Here,
the homeless speak with their hands,
operatic in their motions,
the climate permitting
a slow grandiloquence.
The lemon shark cruising the flats
near Woman Key, startles, as does
the stickleback, gills furiously moving
in the silted green of the tidal marsh.
But days go by

and nothing truly astonishes.
Not the tattooed boy, sleeping
near the Southernmost Point,
not the pot-bellied pig
that tries to mount
our neighbor's Harley Davidson,
not the endless summer sky.
And when a tropical depression
staggers through the Leeward Islands,
we wait it out—
until a disaster that never occurs
brings us "The Hurricane Special,"
its headline asking "Are You Ready?"
A question we've answered
by lingering on,
as the seaplanes fall through the spires
of the Star of the Sea Church,
like spirits driven from heaven,
finding a place to land.

Morning at The Artist's House, Key West

Below the tin roof and pewter sky,
the Czech gardener gathers leaves
from the sapodilla tree.
He sweeps the bricks and trims
the bougainvillea, the coral vine,
the creeping fig. The haze clears,
the sky blues,
the traffic and ring of mopeds
pick up. I hear the gardener
speaking to the maid,
No, no, no, trying to be understood
in a new language. Consider
the Victorian geometry: gray clapboard
and lavender shutters, the haphazard
design—porch over porch, over
added-on rooms—all this,
topped by the octagon
of a silver cupola. To my left,
the tin roof glows.
As if it might be the sky.
As if the roof might be something new
and separate from the sky.
Past the fountain, an iron fence
divides the courtyard
from the walk. In the street,
an orange panel truck,
its paint softened to a dull patina.
The words that once told its use
are blackened out.
The truck awaits some new direction,
the words to say some new use.
A fire truck races by. Then a police siren
can be heard, approaching life or death

from a different angle. Behind me,
on this rooftop deck, a woman
in a blue bathing suit. A cloud rolls
through the parabolic curve
of her sunglasses, green on green
against each plastic lens.

Clearwater

The ocean was on fire when the divers went out, and the water they
swam through was never clear.
  JAMES KALLSTROM, FBI Special Agent-in-Charge,
  New York Field Office

The beach was wide, and there was no hard line
where shore ended and the Gulf began.
I was there for the disaster conference:
lectures and workshops about the lost plane.
You spent mornings at the pool, reading
Newton's *Optics*, sitting behind a screen
that kept you from the wind.
It was late summer,
and storms rumbled across the island,
the arrival and exit of the waves, flattened
and prolonged. Pelicans rose
and the terns, insistent and sharp,
dove toward the blind spot of the skull,
no sweet note among them.

The hotel ballroom was dark,
and the special agent held the lectern,
clicking through the slides.
The front section blew away, he said,
and the body continued to fly.
In the warehouse they are restoring it—
charred skin to a frame.
The charts show the parabola
of a descent, and the isobars of a low,
that gathered and sank into difficult weather.
And yes, there was the work
of recovering the dead.

After dinner, we left the hotel
and drove past the royal palms,
the stink of rotting mangroves
heavy in the air. Behind us,
a storm swept in,
and beyond the squall line,
the sun went flaming into the Gulf.
In the rear-view mirror, I saw it clearly:
The clouds were incandescent,
like walls of fire, rising around
a biblical city, swirling past
the old and new hotels,
a *camera lucida* of rain and fire,
projecting an image
from which a vision might be traced.
An optical illusion, you said,
the saturation of water-in-air,
something about perspective and
a vanishing point. I choose to believe
in what was seen—
to place a finger against the sky
and trace the descent.
Where the finger touches water,
the wreckage enters the sea.
I've never gone to the bottom of the sea.

That night we walked the beach and
on your dare, stripped and ran into the surf.
Unfamiliar stars descended in the sky,
and the Gulf was a caldron, still spinning out
clouds. Beyond the bar, there was
an undertow. In the water, a phosphorescence,
a hand drawn through dragging tracers in its wake,
then the waves washed over and pulled us
from our feet. Our hands parted
and our bodies disappeared.
I should have foreseen this, how

after the storm, the waves would rise
against us. It was the end of summer,
or it was the beginning of fall,
the cusp of something, the epicycle
to a larger loss. The bodies of the dead
had been restored to the living,
and there was no hard line where shore ended
and the Gulf began.

III

After Three-and-a-Half Years with Calypso, Odysseus Says, To Hell with It, I'm Not Going Home

It's the story no one talks about—
how he came to love the nymph—
her tangled braids and open thighs,
the aroma of partridge, roasting
over sweetwood. Ten years
against Troy and the endless journey home.
His men consumed by monsters and the sea.
Then Calypso's island—the grapes
ambered by a noble rot,
and goats bleating on the hillside.
Day after day, the sea rises
and falls. Calypso trills her little song
and Ithaca seems more distant.
Until Homer must go to him,
meet Odysseus on the beach
and explain the narrative—
that he, as author, is the god
who must be obeyed.
It's why the plot stalls out
at the start of Book 5.
Calypso's change of heart
is Homer strumming and chanting
for time, until Odysseus
picks up his ax and walks toward the trees,
cursing the poet's blindness.

Women in Love

for Tony Hoagland

I've never been able to finish it,
so I buy the book on tape,
and drive across Michigan, lost
in the English Midlands.
It's a lovely story, and perhaps my mind
is adrift, but through two-and-a-half cassettes,
no one seems to be in love.
Instead, men get naked to dive into ponds,
and men get naked to wrestle each other.
Not that I mind. No one likes skinny dipping
more than I, though snapping turtles
are a worry for the well-endowed.
And I'm not against naked wrestling,
though if the wrestlers take steroids
they may shrink their nether regions,
causing women to laugh and fall
out of love. I agree, Lawrence is
a holy writer, *el brujo grande,* his
men and women all free and helpless.
But my allergies are acting up, and
I'm thinking about the meeting I'm late for,
and it's only when men get naked that
I listen again, as Gerald and Birkin jujitsu
across the drawing room floor. I'm not
asking for men wrestling women,
but what about *one scene* where a naked woman
flips a naked woman into a shallow pond?
Say, Gudrun against Ursula,
which has the dueling-sisters element,
or either one taking on
that annoying Hermione, giving her
the full-Nelson she deserves. What we

might have seen in the director's cut
of "Tarzan Returns," where Jane tangles
with Benita Hume, in a barely clothed slapfest
for the heart of the Jungle King,
said to have gotten most interesting
in a certain lost reel. But eschew that,
the sneeze-word that says *no.*
This line of thinking has *patriarchal tendencies,*
it appeals to *the prurient interest,*
the first strand of the *Miller* test uncoils
its lascivious tongue across the dash,
and what I truly want is love,
love that is transgendered! Like Tarzan,
every morning, I want to kiss my jungle-bride
awake! Art is *so* savage! Are we
great tumbling beetles, whose horns
have locked, pushing each other forth and
back across some jungle path? Even
Lawrence, who wrote the best sex
in the English language, wasn't too busy
making love, writing it down, and cough, cough,
coughing up blood to mock the dead,
calling Melville a sententious old bore,
and Whitman, worse, a dribbling, oozing, leaker.
This could go on, of course, like lung-snot
in our hankies—this hate business, this
punch-each-other-in-the-nose business,
these salon jealousies, backstabbing
over silver bullets and soggy canapés,
but, like the great hymn urges, *let it begin
with me,* because as I miss my exit
east of Battle Creek, I see the trenches:
Derrida to the left of us, Cleanth Brooks
on the right, Paul deMan—crypto-fascist
or lifelong comsymp?—lobbing a cluster bomb,
and have to ask: Can't we all swing out
on some long jungle vine,

and drop together, thumping our chests
and screaming, into the vast literary pond?
At one time, there was a certain pathos,
an era of good feelings. Michigan hadn't yet
been mapped by the white man,
the lion lay down with the lamb,
and the Midlands still had the mystery
of a wild, dark continent.

Walking Toward the Village

It is the best part, he decides—
their walk after the work is finished,
snow falling and the moon behind the clouds,
full for no particular reason.
For a long while, nothing more
than the sound of two bodies walking,
until she begins a child's verse:
"Here is the church, here is the steeple,"
but moves her hands into a gesture
of supplication, of a priest saying
"Oremus," as the snow goes on with its task,
all ornament and silence.

The Far-Away Rivers

Saturday night at Center Lake
in August 1952. My mother and father
are making love
in the back of a Chevrolet,
a dark car rocking
outside a darkened cottage,
the radio playing big band.
Music is changing, yes,
but Mother is drunk and will always be
a sucker for the Dorsey Brothers.
Father eases out, zips
and lights a Pall Mall,
as a blood moon slumps
into the willows.
Mother lays her head back
and smiles her bleary smile,
her head still nodding
to the music of cola and rum.
Four hundred yards away,
the river begins,
the route that opened a wilderness
to the voyageurs and Astor,
leaving this lake and flowing west
to empty Michigan's palm
like a Heart line, draining
the Plain of Mars.

                ii.

I know where the WPA
cemented the river underground.
The stream bed of weeds and mussel shells

and the blackness of the tunnel,
the slope of concrete
to the bottom of the basin.
We floated paper boats,
tiny ships disappearing
and the river also gone
until it emerged on Loomis Street.
We played hide-and-seek in the park,
my sister calling
Ollie, ollie, oxen-free,
the day of Uncle Benny's wake.
They laid him out in the living room,
and the women made sandwiches
of boiled tongue
and pumpernickel bread,
potato salad and casseroles,
though my Irish uncles, loyal
in this new world
to the forms of the old,
took their consolation
in dark beer and whiskey.

   iii.

The field of grief,
and in winter, the greater field.
For two weeks, snow drifts
against the house,
blowing in off the lake,
up the channel carved
by the river at its mouth,
causing white-outs across the lift bridge.
Today, a melting world.
The snow piles soften
to a child's mountain range,
revealing the dead

and what passes for them.
In what was once our kitchen
you paint a self-portrait,
red flesh-tones and curtain
against a dark backdrop,
the door closing or opening,
a nude woman
seated upon a green couch,
one leg pulled firmly to her breast,
her black eyes staring
directly from the canvas. I am
listening to a Brahms quartet,
and around the violins, viola, and cello
are the sounds you make, painting.

iv.

The deaconess at Holiness Church
pulled the alarm,
the night the machine shop burned.
Sparks and ash swirled down the block,
torching the Mitchells' rose arbor.
Mother bought three cases of beer,
and threw a party for the crowd
milling behind the barricades.
I see her there. The force of light,
refracted through the force of water,
shadows wobbling against the pavement,
orange light firing the glass
of her bottles.

v.

The middle years.
The river flowed through the farmer's field.
There was a mill and a spillway

for the mill. The trees
were emerald green
and reflected on the water.
There is a street that bears my surname
at the foot of the Brooklyn Bridge.
Drunken nights I spent
in the restaurant of the emigres.
Cigars, sevruga, and cognac.
Let us toast your life and health,
Arkady used to say,
Zah vahsheh zdahrovyeh!
Zah vahsheh zdahrovyeh!
Behind the barrier dunes,
the river unravels itself.
I lose myself in this dissembling
and am simply lost for a while.
The story of a man,
adrift at midstream,
pressing music to his head.

   vi.

I remember the Litany of Saints,
the way the dust motes flared
in the rooms of my grandmother's house,
Joseph, the glue-sniffing Ottawa boy,
who built a tree house near the pond
and fell asleep with a paper bag
cradled against his chest.
An old couch sprouting weeds
and the men who searched the field
for empties. The steps between
"Veronica Wipes the Brow of Jesus,"
and "Christ Falls for the Third Time."
A black snake that startled
and dropped into the water.

The swirl of bodies, barely seen
across the surface of a river.

vii.

I'm writing a history of rivers.
Gathered from township records,
recorded in deeds and county plats,
the contracts of loggers
and speculators. A history
of hundred-year floods
and black-powder explosions,
blasting away the beaver dams.
Here, the Swedes lived,
and there, the drunken Irish,
but more than this. This is the valley
where the glaciers retreated,
from which the Sauk withdrew
under pressure from the French.
Here is the cemetery,
and there, the graves of the dead.
And from this hill you may follow
the meander toward the lake.

viii.

An ice jam backs the river through the flood plain.
The crows settle in the haw trees
along the edge of the impoundment.
How many days of silence
before the sonata begins?
The groan of sheet ice,
fracturing against sheet ice,
the geese calling for open water.
I say this goes on,
and when we cross the lift bridge,

you ask whether this
or the dead channel ahead of us
is the river and I say,
No, this is the river,
we are crossing it now.

Cat Descending a Staircase

Because he has shaken
a dream of dead birds
and rises without amends
and returns to a state of grace.
Because he has plans
for the saucer of milk
and knows the night terrain,
or rises, stretches, and has no plans.
Because the mysterious furnace
whispers in the hall, and the moon
is full, and must be regarded
from the back of the living room couch.
Because voices are staggering
outside along the street,
arguing a difference
between solitude and loneliness,
and then one turns
and is about to open the door,
and when it opens, a time of grief
and tiny sighs
will begin in this room.
And despite this,
because it's a form of happiness—
descending through moonlight,
his irises swelling to admit
whatever light there is.

A Recipe in Which My Ex-Wife No Longer Appears

Because rosemary is the herb
of remembrance, I remember
making roast chicken
with rosemary, garlic, and carrots.
It's pointless to ask for the recipe.
I've lost the directions
and can write them now in only
a simple way. I took a roaster
rubbed with lemon,
put two pats of butter
under the skin of the breasts, cut
the carrots on the bias, tossed them
around the bird, with whole cloves
of garlic, salt, and
freshly picked rosemary,
lightly scored with the edge
of a sharp knife.
I added more butter for the carrots,
drizzled olive oil over the skin,
then tumbled the butter and oil
through the carrots, rosemary, and garlic.
The rest of dinner? Perhaps the flowers,
the last of the gladiolas,
pink, red, and a peachy orange,
are a detail borrowed from another time,
though I remember arranging the stems
in an empty blue vase,
one of the few things I kept
when the marriage ended. I
would put on a string quintet,
the liner notes to which read
the brightness of the music is greater
for its knowledge of the dark, as I circled

the room and the redwood deck beyond.
I set the table, put out wine glasses,
forks, plates, the knives,
a loaf of French bread, made a salad
of escarole and green leaf lettuce,
then mixed a vinaigrette, as the house
filled with roasty smells, the garlic and carrots
just beginning to caramelize.
I remember making a fire, uncorking
the wine, a Zinfandel, and yes,
pouring a glass of it, pulling the pan
from the oven, the balsamic,
sweet-and-bitter aroma of rosemary
swelling the room, letting the bird set
and slightly cool, the moment
the knife broke the skin.
Say what you will about me
in that marriage:
faithless, drunk, spendthrift.
My only claims are that I cooked
for her. That's what I knew of love.
And I gave her what she wanted
when she chose a different life.

Rockford in Malibu

Wall-eyed, punch-drunk, pistol-whipped
by age—eight seasons plus reruns,
blow after blow to the head—ran a tab.
His trailer, where every Friday night
hoods came busting through the door,
smells of bacon grease and cigarettes.
The files got packed away
but were never closed. Sometimes
he looks at one and tries to guess
who was the suspect and who was the client.
He wanders through the pickleweed
and marsh dodder, trousers rolled,
torso lost in the polyester
of his coat. Malibu is a sunny place.
The waves turn gently and
sea lions call from the navigation buoys.
At night, he sleeps and does not sleep,
as morning builds slowly in the dark.
Sgt. Becker retired in '86
and sends a card at Christmas.
Rockford thinks of writing back,
but what would he say? *I walk*
to the pier and nap in the afternoon.
I catch sand dabs when the kelp is in
and hum snatches of my theme song.
My kidneys ache. The past is a mystery
I'm still trying to solve.
He heads for the pier, buys some bait,
steadies himself against a picnic table,
dodging terns and cormorants.
When he squints, their shadows come at him,
like blackjacks and gun handles,
falling from the sky.

Domestic Architecture

My house is gray and foursquare,
with a room for books that faces the water.
I can see the south shore, and a concrete bridge
crossing the narrows.

My house is the caretaker's house
on the drive to the old resort.
The hotel burned and wasn't rebuilt.

There are two benches in back
and three Mexican fireplaces.
When the power goes out,
I can see the northern lights.

A trial inventory: 2,000 books, give or take.
A collection of masks,
a desk and bed, framed letters
and photographs, two fly rods.

One hornets' nest each year in the eaves.
Also a bee hive beneath the shingles
in the back.

I saw the crows mob a barred owl.
The owl flew three times within my sight,
uttering a long, hoarse call—an almost human cry
of exasperation and complaint.

There are Chinese fortunes taped to the walls,
quotes from St. Paul and Theodore Roethke.

The cats run wild, and the dogs want
a walk across the bridge or to the place

where, years ago, weedy channels were dug
into the lake, breaking the close.

In the field next door—a rusty barrel,
and a pile of mussel shells
scraped from the hull of a fishing boat.

I found a dead bird on the doorstep—
a mourning dove, breast open to the heart.

At the old hotel, Edgar Lee Masters
decided to quit lawyering and write poems.
"Whenever I look at a law book," he said,
"I have to lie down." A year later,
he built the house beyond the hill
and wrote *Spoon River*.

I have music. I'm going to walk circles
around the yard, *Sonny Rollins, Volume 1,*
playing on the stereo.

I buried a dead cat under the hemlock.
Another cat, brother of the deceased,
sleeps atop the grave.

During storms, I stand out in the wind
and stare at the house from various angles.
The house is wrapped in cedar shingles,
the finest thing against the weather.

Three kegs of nails in the basement, left
when the caretaker died. I think he meant
to build a larger life.

Fidelity

I woke up when the rain began.
The hot August night and a storm
blowing in across the lake.
The lightning started,
and the wild hosannas of the trees.
I went to close the windows on the porch,
then opened the door to watch the rain,
ponding in the yard and the street beyond.
The lightning lit up and lit up the air,
brilliant and incendiary. Then
the shock of thunder, answering
and rolling away.
Had anyone been looking,
it might have startled them—
the body of a man, suddenly framed
in an open doorway.
But I wanted the mist
and the cooling breeze of the storm.
I walked back to the bedroom
and found you awake in the dark.
"Where did you go?" you asked,
fright and sleep searching for balance
in your voice.
And lightning lit up our room
where I stood leaning against
the frame of the door, while the rain
went on, falling and
falling in the dark of the yard.

Hornets' Nest

It was lying next to my truck,
still gathered around a branch
from the oak tree behind the garage.
The nest had cracked and sentinels rose
through the jagged open seam.
This explained why we couldn't eat
in the yard last summer.
Whenever we tried,
hornets would descend
and attack whatever was sweetest:
an orange, the succulence
of watermelon, the tartness of an apple.
Gleaming black-and-yellow abdomens
throbbing against the china,
antennae furiously turning, as if the air
told them something about us,
permitted them to judge and find us wanting.
Late for work, yes, but I looked into the nest.
I saw the paper comb,
and where the walls had torn apart,
I saw the unhatched eggs.

I once knew a girl
who'd been given too much in life.
Her mother was from Charleston
and spoke with a drawl,
though they'd lived here for years.
They were rich, with a big house
on the lake, full of art and expensive things.
I was young and had nothing to speak of,
but this was when I *wanted* a great deal,
this was when I had that desire.
I can't say why I was there that afternoon,

and forget what the girl had done
to get into so much trouble:
run up the balance on her mother's credit card,
or piled the Audi into a bridge
after a party with her friends.

I remember an argument.
The mother starting it. As if to say,
I will embarrass you in front of someone
who means nothing to us.
And the daughter egging her on,
giving back even better than she got.
Finally, the mother, losing her drawl,
called her daughter,
"a goddamned hornets' nest."
The daughter laughed, then walked
out of that elegant house. For all I know,
out of that elegant life.

                    What does it take
to get a hornets' nest out of your life?
I thought of everything. Smashing it with rocks,
torching it with lighter fluid, driving the truck
over it. In the end I waited
for a cold rain
and let the water collapse the pod
into something dark and harmless.
Now days go by and nothing pursues us.
I don't know why I would want
our lives to be different.
But imagine a photograph, taken
as it fell. Caught in the flash, swelling the dark
between earth and the tree—
that might have been something
I truly wanted. It explains everything,
this enduring want. Walking into the world,
telling it all.

Comet

Tonight, you throw your body
across the couch,
and pronounce *Boring,*
as though claiming a new planet.
You sulk and curse and,
told to watch your tongue,
choose exile, the rest of us sighing
tiny sighs of relief—
the surly boy growing so awkwardly
into a man's body,
is finally gone from the room.
After midnight, I get up.
Now you are entirely gone.
In your bedroom, the window open
and television on,
casting a blue glow.
I imagine your escape,
skateboarding through the dark
of an empty parking lot.
There are names for your maneuvers
that are lost on me.
Just as I have no words
for what each of us endures,
or in youth or age, thinks we do.
I walk into the yard and light
this first cigarette.
Above me, a comet has returned,
silvered and still,
that hasn't passed
in some 4,000 years.

During National Poetry Month

In the Chicago Public Library,
a man is reading a poem about leeks.
Over his left shoulder, in a third-floor window
of the building across the street, a light
is glowing. The light is large and shaped
like a 7, as if I see the lintel and one jamb
of a glowing doorway.
I decide the light is the color of a leek,
where the white of the head merges
with the green of the stem.

The light wavers in the window-glass.
When Edward Hopper was old, there were days
he had trouble painting a straight line,
and on those shakier days he mixed
more white into his colors, blurring his line,
softening the light he worked into the canvas.
The window has that effect.
And something strange: Through the wavery frame
a woman in black begins circling, seeming to
step through the pale green doorway
again and again, the warped glass distorting
her body differently each time.

The poet finishes reading, looks up,
and begins another poem, this one
about pears, just as the woman stops
circling, steps to the window and,
hands on her hips, looks down and across,
into the second-floor window of the Chicago
Public Library. And *yes,* the light of the doorway
is the light of a pear's skin, and the light
flooding the street—, the brandied light

of Calvados, and the woman could be
one of Hopper's women, beautiful and
imperfect, the breasts too large or an arm
too thick, as he sometimes caught them:
stepping toward the frame, leaning out
into the world.

Mythe

There is a couple with a baby
in the office next door, and the man
is wailing. *That's a mythe!* he says,
That is a total mythe! The woman
says again, *He can't care for no baby,*
and in a lull when I can barely hear
the murmur of the caseworker's voice,
I finally understand the man
has mispronounced the word *myth,*
making the *y* long, and he means
what the woman says is *untrue,*
that it is *a story, belief, or notion*
commonly held to be true,
but utterly without a factual basis.

The man loves her.
His love is more dangerous
than no love at all.
What he wants is their life,
before she met the ladies of Holiness Church,
who came to the trailer
after he tried to kill himself.
By the time he was out of the psych ward,
his clothes and one armchair
were packed in the bed of his truck.
Last week, he wandered into the evening service,
breaking through the rink-a-tink
of an old Wesleyan hymn, shouting
I won't have that baby raised
in a snake-handler church!

I make a note to call Protective Services—
ask them to visit the woman and child,
then check out the cabin
where the man claims to live.
I think of other files.
Of a schizophrenic,
who dropped two sons
into a smoldering foundry ladle,
saying they would be better off burning
in this world, than the one that waits
beyond.

Now there is a disturbance, shouting
and a chair scraping back.
The man has taken the baby
and run into the hall. When I stop him,
he slides to the floor, the child,
almost asleep, dressed
in a dirty blue snow suit,
arms and legs splayed flat
against the man's chest.
I am trying to live a biblical life!
the woman yells at the caseworker,
as the man, inexplicably, rises,
hands the baby over like a small blue doll,
and walks out.
I cannot say whether the look he gives me
is something unuttered,
or nothing at all.
This is not what he wants,
or the end of the story.

Charon in August

for Jack Ridl

The languid afternoon. Insects,
droning on into the night. Charon lies
at the bottom of his rowboat,
thinking about his life.
No classes this summer. No deliveries
to the other side. That's fine with him.
And if he's no longer wraith-like,
he can handle that. He's grown a little bald,
a touch of gray in the beard now, yes,
but still cuts a romantic figure.
Past the golden light of dusk, into
the growing darkness, he listens to the river
push against the gunwales. How many poets,
he wonders, have I ferried across this river?
Vergil, Homer, Horace, Ovid, Lucan.
Dante himself, who passed out
after too many "drinkies" at the airport,
and had to be loaded by hand
into Charon's boat. Then the endless stream
of acolytes, showing up after the readings
for the parties at his house. Eating
Charon's nacho chips, drinking all his beer,
Cerberus yowling apoplectically in the yard.
And the local bards! My God,
their egos! He's tired of hearing
about so-and-so's grant application,
and the terrific contract that one got
with Graywolf or Knopf.
He thinks about Jesus though and smiles
despite himself. There was a poet!
He showed up late, weird story about the trip,
stigmata leaking all over the boat.

Spent three days in bed
with *delerium tremens*, then flew off
to collect a genius grant.
"In the middle of my life,
in the middle of my life . . ."
Isn't that what Dante kept muttering,
nursing a glass of pinot noir,
after speaking to Charon's seminar
on disembodied poetics?
Charon mouths these same words,
touches his hand gently to his forehead,
snuggles back against the bottom of the boat.
Feeling kind of hungry, he thinks.
Wonder if Mrs. Charon wants to step out
for a bite. Maybe some ribs.
He knows this all night barbecue
near the bridge to Circle 6. He feels a twitch,
and shifts his weight against the keel.
What did his chiropractor say?
A swollen disk, amid
the lower lumbar vertebrae.
Not going to pole so hard
he decides, lays his head back
and closes his eyes. Just resting.
Perhaps the tiniest cat nap. Slowly,
his breathing slows. Above him the stars,
not yet fixed,
twist into funny animal shapes,
like a clown's balloons,
testing their myths across the sky.

Calling the Code

I'm forty-six and beyond a life
of crises. No more foreclosures,
drink or drugs,
walks on the pier with the ocean calling.
Even my son, who vanished
atop a skateboard alleyed through the dark,
rides back on a mountain bike,
sworn to a clean life,
license thankfully lost
in a drunk driving mix-up in Colorado.
He's training to be an *executive chef.*
I'm not trying to prove anything,
he says, over a cup of French roast
with a shot of espresso,
a shot in the dark, he calls it.
But lately, I feel like Richard Nixon,
our worst chief executive,
on the steps of his helicopter,
throwing both hands in the air—
the familiar *v.* A signal
we're leaving the REM stage
of a long national nightmare.
I gave 'em the resignation sign,
he said, in that loathsome book,
My Nine Crises—Watergate,
the enemies list, that good Republican cloth coat,
bombing Cambodia
into a land of muddy sticks.
Still, didn't you feel for him, lifting
over the White House that final day?
Nothing to come but those broody years
walking the beach at San Clemente,
pants rolled up his phlebitic calves,

mumbling about the splendors
of The Forbidden City. And to certain people,
I *am* a kind of Tricky Dick—
the cranky man in the junky house
at the far-end of the bridge—
volume at 10 on Mozart's *Requiem*.
I'm not trying to prove anything, but
my crises were legion, a legion of pigs
sent squealing off a cliff.
They made everyone *so tired*. So, nine
or ninety, who's counting? Not me, not even
the night my heart fluttered
like a bird dragged home by the cat—
awake in the dark with night sweats,
unable to breathe, my arm gone numb.
When they inserted the IV, when they taped
the monitor to my chest,
I slipped into a reverie, a peaceful dream, really,
of a diner in the American desert:
night, the place almost empty.
My son is the fry cook, flipping
eggs, chatting up the waitress.
I ask for *a shot in the dark*.
"Ain't got any," she says,
"Just regular or decaf."
"That's my son," I tell her. She smiles,
says, "He's a good kid," and takes my order:
two eggs over easy, toast and coffee, ham
on the side. Everything you need
to clog the heart. And it's *good*—
the kid can cook—the best I've ever had.
I pay, and as I crunch across
the parking lot, I look up.
It's *Marine One*, beating west
into the night.
In the strobes, I see Dick's face—
sweaty, needing a shave.

He throws both hands up and shoots me
our secret sign, as I come-to for a moment,
thinking, *Next time through,*
I want the scram-slam, next time through,
I want pineapple juice and the breakfast fajitas.
I'm flat on my back, they are calling the code,
we are flying over the bridge.

Age of Consent

To the chair near the linden tree,
where my daughter once wept
and could not be consoled.
To the black-and-white cat,
carrying a sparrow into the garage.
To a February thaw
and to every small act of mercy.
To the light that floods the anchor of the bridge.
To the walnut trees aligned in a dolorous row
and the man who tried to make order of this.
To middle age and the condition of my heart.
To the Tibetan prayer for the dead
and the Episcopalian service
for those lost at sea.
To the split oak stacked
against the ramshackle house
and the fires that will carry me
through another winter.
To the whiskey I am allowed in dreams.
To the fiction of my life
and whatever truth I've made of it.
To what the hand finds
when laid against the wall, in the very place
where the bees have made their hive,
some great buzzing heart,
alive again beneath the lath.

Last Walk with Sinatra's Dog

The Odyssey, Book 11, lines 138–157

Sinatra rises while Barbara is still asleep,
snaps the leash onto Satchmo's collar,
picks up the oar he's kept in the garage
and steps out into the desert.
At first, Satchmo mouths the lead, tail
wagging, eager for a walk.
But as they go beyond the curvy drives,
beyond the last of the flat-roofed architecture,
the dog drops the leash,
from time-to-time balancing on three legs
to mark the trail. He looks back
and smiles a doggy-smile: *the years together,*
after so many years apart. The sun arcs
into the cloudless sky, and Sinatra
pulls out a pair of shades. His breath
is labored. He begins to sweat.
But he shifts the oar and walks on,
until the golf course and condos
straggle into nothingness. He slows
among the jacaranda and mesquite
and looks back. The horizon blurs—
sea-like, oceanic, though there's no sea
but the Salton Sea, vast saline relic
of the orange groves and water-schemes,
there, somewhere in the distance.
Sinatra lays down the oar
and begins piling stones around it.
He works slowly, propping it up,
until the oar rises, blade against the sky,
the oar of a boat he rowed as a child,
skimming the mussel flats of Hoboken.
He lights a cigarette and thinks of the lost.

No more *Sinatra looks deeply into her eyes.*
Never again *Sinatra takes a final sip*
and moves to center stage. He begins
a Johnny Mercer song, as he picks up
the lead and pats the dog. *Sky lark,*
he sings, *have you anything to say to me?*
And Satchmo joins in, moaning sadly on
the exhale, as they resume the long walk,
back down the valley
toward the house in Palm Springs.

The Brittingham Prize in Poetry

THE UNIVERSITY OF WISCONSIN PRESS POETRY SERIES

RONALD WALLACE, GENERAL EDITOR

Places/Everyone • Jim Daniels
C. K. Williams, Judge, 1985

Talking to Strangers • Patricia Dobler
Maxine Kumin, Judge, 1986

Saving the Young Men of Vienna • David Kirby
Mona Van Duyn, Judge, 1987

Pocket Sundial • Lisa Zeidner
Charles Wright, Judge, 1988

Slow Joy • Stefanie Marlis
Gerald Stern, Judge, 1989

Level Green • Judith Vollmer
Mary Oliver, Judge, 1990

Salt • Renée Ashley
Donald Finkel, Judge, 1991

Sweet Ruin • Tony Hoagland
Donald Justice, Judge, 1992

The Red Virgin: A Poem of Simone Weil • Stephanie Strickland
Lisel Mueller, Judge, 1993

The Unbeliever • Lisa Lewis
Henry Taylor, Judge, 1994

Old & New Testaments • Lynn Powell
Carolyn Kizer, Judge, 1995